The

Little Book

of

Reflexology

The Little Book of Reflexology

by

Michelle R. Kluck

Running Press
Philadelphia • London

Library of Congress Cataloging-in-Publication Number 2001087094

ISBN 0-7624-1088-4
This book may be ordered by mail from the publisher.
Please include $1.00 for postage and handling.
But try your bookstore first!

Running Press Book Publishers
125 South Twenty-second Street
Philadelphia, Pennsylvania 19103-4399

Log on to www.specialfavors.com to order
Running Press Miniature Editions™ with your
own custom-made covers!

Visit us on the web!
www.runningpress.com

Contents

Part I:

An
Introduction
to
Reflexology

Reflexology is an ancient healing art and a holistic healing technique that aims to treat the body, mind, and spirit. Reflexology is an integrative health science that does not isolate a disease and treat its symptoms, but rather supports the whole person by nurturing a state of balance and harmony. It tries to get to the root of the disease. This gentle therapy encourages the body to heal itself at its own pace, often counteracting a lifetime of misuse.

The art of reflexology is not the same as a foot massage or massage therapy. Rather than simply rubbing randomly, reflexology treats the feet as a microcosm of the entire body. It is based on the theory that there are zones and reflex areas in the feet and hands, which correspond to all glands, organs, and systems of the body. By applying pressure using thumb, finger, and hand techniques to these reflex areas, you can relax and rejuvenate every part of the body, reduce stress, and promote physiological changes to improve your overall well-being. Reflexology can naturally conquer many health

problems, and also serves as a form of preventative maintenance. It's a safe, easy, and beneficial method of treatment that can help you take responsibility for and become more intimately involved with your own health. What's more, it heightens your own body awareness.

The human body is highly intelligent and has a remarkable, built-in, self-correcting system that can restore health to diseased areas. The goal of reflexology, in effect, is to re-educate, re-pattern, and re-condition nerves so that the body can heal itself by using that self-correcting system. Better still, reflexol-

ogy is a safe, non-invasive, complementary health practice that facilitates on-going physical, emotional, and spiritual improvements.

Reflexology vs. Massage

While both reflexology and massage share the same goal, which is to enhance the well being of the client, they are two different modalities with their own individual strengths. Although both involve the use of the hands to apply their techniques, there are several important differences between the two disciplines:

1. Massage is the systematic manipulation of soft tissues of the body, while reflexology is the application of specific pressure to reflex points in the hands and feet. The effect of reflexology is seen at a distance from where the pressure is applied; its intent is not to change the soft tissue of the body.

2. Massage works through the musculature, while reflexology works through the nervous system.

3. Massage employs many different types of strokes to directly affect specific areas of the body, while reflexology uses on and off pressure with the thumbs and fingers to indi-

rectly stimulate many areas that an individual might not otherwise be able to affect.

What Can Reflexology Do for Me?

Reflexology has been found to be beneficial for a wide range of disorders, including headaches, sinus congestion, stiffness in the back and neck, digestion, and hormonal problems.

Additionally, reflexology can bring you soothing stress relief and relax not only your feet, but your entire body. It can improve circulation,

ease pain, and boost energy. Most people who try reflexology find they benefit from it to some degree; the problem either clears up completely or the symptoms decrease. The treatment can be extremely relaxing and pleasurable to receive, as well as stimulating and invigorating.

Benefits of Reflexology

1. Stress Relief

Whether you suffer from insomnia, chronic fatigue, stomach problems, or migraines, the root of many common health problems can be linked to stress. Stress can be caused by mental, emotional, physical, or environmental factors, and in this fast-paced society, it's almost impossible to avoid it completely. Stress can be quite damaging to the body and mind. It's well known that an individual trying to function while under the influence of prolonged stress is less capable of defending

against illnesses and repairing damage caused by injury.

Since reflexology is primarily a relaxation technique, it can counteract the effects of stress as it helps the body relax. Through the relaxation process, the body is more capable of dealing with the stresses placed on it by daily living and strains associated with illness. Reflexology gently nudges the body toward better functioning by relaxing the muscles, encouraging better circulation, and improving the functions of all body systems to promote better overall outlooks (when you feel good, it's much easier to be positive).

It's safe to say that stress, which can make us age more quickly and become physically ill and emotionally upset, is the enemy. Reflexology, on the other hand, can become a friend you have right at your fingertips!

2. Muscle Relaxation

Many factors besides stress can cause your muscles to tighten up.Too much time spent sitting in one position, holding a phone or heavy bag on the same side, working out with weights, and emotional problems are but a few common causes. Whatever the source may be, when your muscles are tense

and overstressed, the energy in your body is thrown off balance. Specifically, the energy in the nerve pathway that connects those muscles with the rest of your body becomes congested. This can lead to fatigue, pain, irritability, and worst of all, more stress.

By stimulating the reflex areas to the parts of the body that are stressed, reflexology can help unblock the energy in the nerves and relax your muscles. Consider for a moment: There are over 7,000 nerves in your feet! By touching these nerves (i.e. rubbing the whole foot) you can affect the reflex areas

in the entire body. This then restores physical harmony and relieves a lot of unwanted and unhealthy muscle tension.

3. Circulation Improvement

In order for all of the body's systems to function properly, it's essential for blood to circulate and reach every cell. The blood carries nutrients and oxygen to the tissues and if, for some reason, the blood can't reach a specific area, the cells in that area will starve and die. When you are stressed, your breathing often becomes shallow and the circulation of blood becomes slug-

gish. As a result, the tissues can become oxygen–deprived, the energy in your body depleted and unstable, and all of your body systems suffer.

To keep your body's circulation running smoothly, reflexology encourages steady blood flow to and from the heart. This improves the flow of oxygenated blood to all of your cells, which then rejuvenates tired tissues and delivers proper nutrition to them.

4. Detoxify and Cleanse

Getting rid of waste and toxins is extremely important to your health. The human body has built–in systems to process and eliminate what

it does not need, and it's necessary for good health that these systems remain unblocked. When the lymphatic, urinary, or intestinal systems are blocked due to a buildup of toxins and waste, the energy in the body stagnates. You may feel lethargic, bloated, and even sick. When you "can't go" it's a terrible feeling. To maintain a healthy, unblocked body you must get rid of the garbage that can damage your system. Reflexology can encourage your body to "let go" and eliminate toxins and waste that upset your body and your mood!

5. Body Systems Balancer

Balance is vital to being healthy in body, mind, and spirit. For the body to keep running smoothly, it strives to maintain a state of homeostasis, which is equilibrium among the various functions and chemical compositions of fluids and tissues. A balance of energy in the body is also crucial to good health. When there is a malfunction in some area of the body, it is natural for the balance in that area to be thrown off. Every part of the body is interconnected, so when there is an imbalance in one area, it almost always leads to an imbalance in another. It's sort of like

a complex, foreign car; when one thing goes wrong, it starts the domino effect and one thing after another goes wrong. To fix the car, you must start from the beginning and repair the damage from the first problem outward. That's reflexology's goal— to promote and sustain balance in every organ, gland, muscle, tissue, and system of the body starting from the source of a problem and moving outward. By relaxing the muscles and sending healing energy throughout the body, reflexology can reestablish and stabilize a healthy equilibrium.

6. Vitality Renewal

Most people don't have enough energy. Individuals who suffer from low levels of energy may find that everything is exhausting and most things, including people, seem to suck what little energy you do have right out of you. Like a battery that needs to be recharged, your body, mind, and spirit also need recharging occasionally.

Energy flows through the universe and it is always available when you need it. You have seven primary energy centers, or chakras, in your body, and at any given moment any one of them may be suffering from a lack of

energy or an imbalance in energy flow. Reflexology can help by sending new energy through the chakras to the whole body, rejuvenating and invigorating every cell of your being. This new vitality can open congested energy pathways, stimulate your spirit, and bring a new level of consciousness to your life.

7. Pain Relief

Whenever you feel pain anywhere in your body, your brain is sending you a signal that something is wrong. Normally, when medication is used to relieve pain, the pain may disappear but the problem is still

there. This can do even more harm to the body because the warning signals from the brain are blocked. For example, if you take a painkiller to relieve the pain from a sprained ankle, you will continue to walk as usual without feeling the twinges of pain that are your body's way of saying, "Don't put any weight on this ankle."

Consequently, you may do more damage because you cannot "hear" this natural warning.

Reflexology is a natural painkiller. By focusing on specific reflex areas, unblocking the pathways where energy may be stuck, and balancing

the energy in the rest of the body, reflexology can effectively relieve pain and send healing energy to the rest of the body. However, don't ignore your aches and pains. Use reflexology as a temporary helper and then get busy finding out what's causing the problem!

8. Early Problem Detection

Have you ever heard the phrase, "If it ain't broke, don't fix it"? Reflexology is preventative health care that aims to strengthen the body so that it doesn't get to the point where you have to "fix" it. By understanding the reflex areas of the

feet and their connection to corresponding body parts, you can determine when something in the body is out of balance and may be malfunctioning (often by detecting a grainy area in the reflex point). Employing reflexology for those detected problem areas clears energy blockages that may contribute to the problem and may also prevent future blockages.

9. Nurtures Loving Relationships

Touch is a very powerful element in human bonding. For babies, it's essential to their survival. Unfortun-

ately, it's often lacking in today's high-tech, fast-paced world. Reflexology can bring the power of touch into daily life, and help couples spend intimate, relaxing, and therapeutic time together.

You don't have to be a massage therapist to be able to bring relaxation and stress relief to someone else. Even a five-minute foot treatment can convey how much you care and can strengthen your relationship. What's more, reflexology offers a technique that stimulates the sex organs and can heat things up in the bedroom. Why not give it a try?

Why Work on the Feet?

The feet often take a severe beating as we cram them into shoes that are too tight and proceed to walk for miles, creating self-induced foot problems for the sake of "a pretty shoe." One of the most important reasons to work on the feet is to give them some relief from the torture they habitually endure and provide a positive support system for the entire body. Additionally, there are several more reasons why you should use foot reflexology:

1. The feet are the least vulnerable part of the body. **The feet are the farthest body part from the head, which is naturally the most vulnerable part of the body. Therefore, those who are uncomfortable with conventional massage may find this technique less threatening and more "user friendly." We see a particularly positive response in babies who cannot always accept other forms of stimulation.**

2. Poor circulation. **Since the feet are the farthest body part from the head, they are susceptible to poor circulation. People who suffer from poor circulation may have cold,**

tender, or swollen hands and feet. Stimulating them with reflexology can improve circulation and encourage the flow of blood to the extremities.

3. Toxin buildup. As we walk around, gravity pushes the toxins in our body down to our feet. The effects of gravity, combined with poor circulation, can lead to the build–up of inorganic waste materials, such as uric acid and calcium crystals, in the soles of the feet. These toxins form "grainy" areas in our feet that are often tender to the touch. These areas aren't hard to find, since they have a very different feel from the rest of the foot.

Besides being a sign of waste build-up, they serve a purpose in that they frequently indicate a problem with the corresponding organ.

Is Reflexology Ever Not Recommended?

Since reflexology treats the whole person, not just the symptoms of the disease, it can help everyone stay balanced and strong. While historically, reflexology has been found to have a positive effect on the body suffering from a wide variety of chronic problems, it is not a solution for all ills. Though reflexology can do no harm, there are three conditions of which you should remain aware and cautious:

1. Thrombosis, the formation of a blood clot in a blood vessel, is a condition that might be aggravated by reflexology, since stimulation might move the clot.

2. Diabetes is a condition that often requires insulin to balance blood sugar levels. Since reflexology can stimulate the pancreas to produce insulin, it may affect the body's insulin level and change the effect of the prescribed amount.

3. Avoid reflexology during the first three months of pregnancy and use caution while pregnant, as labor

can be induced by direct and strong stimulation of the reflex areas to the reproductive organs.

In addition, reflexology is not recommended in the case of serious systemic diseases, where increased circulation might cause the infection to spread, and also in the case of injuries to the feet. If you have any specific concerns about the safety of reflexology, consult your physician. Reflexology can be used as a complement to any type of medical approach or therapy, but it is not intended as a substitute for medical treatment.

Part II:

The Approach: How to Treat the Feet

For each person, the treatment and effect of reflexology are unique. Since no two bodies are the same, every reflexology treatment is different as it is always adjusted to meet the needs of the individual. In this sense, reflexology is holistic and somewhat intuitive. If you only have a few moments to work, I suggest you go right to "problem" areas. If you're working on yourself, you can usually tell where your feet are tender and where you need to focus

your attention. If you're working on someone else, the best thing to do is to ask them what part of their body, if any, may be bothering them and start from there. Ask them to let you know if you hit any tender areas so that you can concentrate there. And by all means, don't overlook your instincts when working on yourself or others. If you suddenly feel like you should spend more time on a spot, do so!

On those occasions when you have more time, there are several different ways to treat the feet. Here are a few different techniques:

1. First–aid. Treat specific symptoms: If you (or your partner) are aware of symptoms of stress in your body, you can go directly to the specific corresponding reflex areas to alleviate the symptoms. For example, if you're suffering from a headache, before you work on any other area of the foot, go directly to the big toe to stimulate the reflex area to the brain and ease headache pain. Sometimes this can bring immediate relief. Go to Part V for an extensive list of common problems and the corresponding reflex areas used to relieve those symptoms and strengthen the body.

2. **Treat a system.** If you know that you (or your partner) are experiencing problems with one particular body system, such as the gastrointestinal or the reproductive system, you can stimulate that whole area on the feet to affect that system in its entirety. With this approach, you may have to work different areas on each foot, since the organs involved in each system may be on different feet.

3. **Full foot workout.** To strengthen each and every part of the body, stimulate the entire foot. The methodical way to do this is to use the four horizontal lines that divide

the foot into five separate areas, and work one area at a time.

To give the foot a full treatment, begin at the heel of the foot and stimulate the area between the heel and the pelvic line. You can use any of the techniques described in Part III. Next, stimulate the area between the pelvic line and the waist line, then the area between the waist line and the diaphragm line. Move on to stimulate the area between the diaphragm line and the neck and shoulder line, then the area from the neck and shoulder line to the tops of the toes.

Things to Remember:

1. Keep your hands soft.

Try to keep your hands relaxed and soft when you touch the feet. Remember, the intention of reflexology is to strengthen the body's own healing abilities by relaxing and de–stressing the body. If you can maintain this focus, your touch will convey the energy necessary to clear energy blockages and soothe the body and mind. This is hard to do if your hands irritate the skin!

2. Communicate.

If you're working on yourself,

you'll know when you hit a sensitive area and you need to lighten your pressure. When you're working on someone else, you'll have to rely on your intuition and good communication to know how to adjust. In the beginning of a treatment, it's important to ask your partner how the pressure you are using feels to them. Tell them to let you know if, at any time, your finger pressure is too hard or painful. Remember, reflexology should feel good. If someone is tensing up because it hurts, much of the positive effect is eliminated.

Take your time and explore as you work. If you come across "grainy" or

tender areas, gently work on these areas for several minutes. Usually with a little extra attention, the tenderness disappears.

3. Feel the foot.

As you apply the reflexology techniques to the feet, don't forget to tune in to your own sense of touch. The more you practice, the easier it will become to find those areas that feel "grainy." These are important since they indicate potential problems with the corresponding organ. As you develop more sensitivity in your fingertips, you'll be able to detect subtle changes in the

surface of the skin and rub out problems before they manifest in the body. Even if you already know that a specific problem exists, by paying attention to what your fingers are feeling, rather than just going through the movements of the technique, you'll be able to give a more effective reflexology treatment.

4. Use your intuition.

There is no precise routine for a reflexology treatment, and there are many ways to relieve a problem. The best thing to do if you are giving a full foot treatment is to focus your energy where you sense there is

congestion. Although this may seem difficult at first, the more you let your fingers move to where they want, the easier it will be to trust your own intuition. Sometimes, you may feel areas on the foot that are warmer or colder than others. This is a sign of possible congestion in the area. Other times, you may just have a "hunch" to work a certain reflex area. Often, if you ask the person you are working on if they have any problems with the corresponding part of their body, they will confirm your intuition.

5. "Grainy" or tender areas.

After a few practice treatments and as your fingers become more sensitive, you'll be able to detect "grainy" areas on the soles of the feet. These are the crystalline deposits of calcium and uric acid that develop at the base of the nerves when there is an imbalance of energy in the nerve pathway. If you find one, spend several minutes working on this area, trying to break down the crystals. By working on these points you can release blockages and restore the free flow of energy to the whole body.

This may feel tender or even a little painful to the person you are working on. But eventually, the graininess disappears and with it, the tenderness and pain also disappear. I always tell people to drink lots of water after a reflexology treatment, because the body needs to eliminate the toxins that the reflexology just released from the base of the nerves. A hot bath after a reflexology treatment is also beneficial.

6. Ticklish feet.

The feet are areas of the body that are not often touched, and many

people are ticklish when you touch the soles of their feet. Usually, it's a light, feathery touch that makes people squirm, giggle, and instinctively pull their feet away. If someone is ticklish, you can usually get beyond the "squirmy" stage by first holding his foot firmly between both of your hands for about ten seconds. This allows him to get used to the sensations of your touch, and relax. Next, as you begin to stimulate the foot, try to keep the pressure firm and your movements small. The best technique for ticklish people is to simply apply direct pressure with your thumbs on specific reflex areas.

If the ticklish person is able to handle thumb pressure, you can add small circles with your thumb moving very slowly. As you feel the foot relax, you can try other reflexology techniques. Just remember to keep your finger pressure firm and your movements slow.

7. Keeping in touch.

In a reflexology treatment, there is an exchange of energy between you, the giver, and the receiver (even if the receiver is you). When you begin a treatment and your hands touch the feet, a physical, mental, emotional, and spiritual connection

begins. If possible, try to maintain this connection throughout the treatment by always keeping one hand on the feet. Even if you have to take a break, or are interrupted for some reason, just keep "in touch" with one hand. This touch will sustain the energetic ex-change so you don't become disconnected with yourself or your partner.

Locating Specific
Reflex Areas

In order to locate specific reflex
areas, it's useful to understand the
four lines that divide the foot and
the body. Each foot is divided horizontally and vertically into five
areas, which correspond to certain
areas of the body.

Each foot is also divided into five
vertical zones, running from the toes
to the heel, which correspond to five
zones of the body. You can locate
specific reflex points on the foot by
studying these divisions and zones

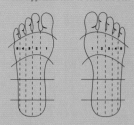

and understanding the areas of the body to which they correspond. The area on the feet above the neck and shoulder line corresponds to every part of the body on or above this line, including the head, eyes, ears, brain, and neck. The area above the diaphragm line corresponds to every

part of the body between the shoulders and diaphragm, including the chest, heart, lungs and shoulders. The area below the diaphragm line corresponds to organs between the diaphragm and waist, including the upper abdominal organs, spleen, and kidneys. The area between the waist line and pelvic line corresponds to organs below the waist, including the lower abdominal organs, bladder, colon, and intestines.

Finally, the area below the pelvic line corresponds to the pelvic area, appendix, sigmoid colon, and sciatic nerve. The inner (medial) edge of the foot corresponds to the spine.

And the outer (lateral) edge corresponds to the arm, shoulder, hip, leg, and knee. The ankle corresponds to the pelvic area, including the reproductive organs.

Part III:

Reflexology
Techniques

Before you begin a reflexlogy treatment, take a minute to clear your mind and focus your energy on the intention to bring relaxation and peace. Rub your hands together to create some heat. (There's nothing nice about having someone touch your feet with ice—cold hands!) Take both feet in your hands and just hold them. Take one or two deep breaths, relax, and exhale slowly. Now you're ready to begin. Work on one foot at a time. Try to stimulate one foot

completely and then switch to the other. You may find that you'll need to stimulate different areas on each foot. Or, you can do the same routine on both feet. Begin by taking one foot in your hands.

Holding the Foot

It's important to support the foot properly for the techniques to be as effective as possible. Throughout a reflexology treatment, the hands will be working together in complementary functions. One hand is the "working hand," which is the hand that applies pressure, and the other is the "supporting hand," which

braces the foot. If you're right-handed, the right hand would be your working hand. The technique I find most comfortable is placing the supporting hand behind the foot, with fingers on the top of the foot and the thumb on the sole of the foot. This way, the foot is stabilized and you can use your other hand to apply pressure.

Rotation (Ankles and Toes)

I always try to warm the foot up before beginning the deeper, finger pressure techniques. Support the foot by placing one hand under the heel, then use the other hand to

slowly rotate the ankle in one direction and then the other. This increases flexibility in the ankle. Next, take each toe between your thumb and index finger and gently roll it back and forth. This relaxing technique wakes up the toes and increases flexibility. It also releases tension in the neck and shoulder area.

Achilles Tendon Stretch

This gentle stretch increases flexibility in the Achilles tendon, which is at the back of the heel, and improves circulation. Support the foot by cupping the heel with one hand. Gently flex the toes backwards

and forwards. Next, pull the top of the foot toward you. The heel will move back slightly. Release this stretch and slowly flex the whole foot back and hold it there for two seconds. Repeat this entire process several times to awaken the foot (just as you stretch your arms in the morning to wake up).

Side-to-Side Ankle Loosening

This is a technique to relax the ankle and calf muscles, and stimulate circulation. Turn your hands up so that the palms face the ceiling, and place the outer edges of your hands (the

"pinkie" sides) on either side of the foot. Gently move your hands left and right, moving up the foot and then down to the heel. The foot should shake from side to side. Do this several times to loosen ankle joints, which reflect the flexibility of all the joints in the entire body. A relaxed ankle reflects a relaxed body.

Spinal Twist

I like to use this relaxing technique at the beginning of every reflexology treatment, even the five–minute quickies. This technique can relax the entire spine and relieve stress throughout the body. Place both

hands side by side on the top of the foot, with the fingers close together and thumbs on the sole of the foot. The hand that is closest to the ankle is the supporting hand, which stabilizes the foot. The hand closer to the toes is the working hand, which moves up the foot towards the toes. The webbing between your thumb and index finger of this hand should lie on the inner edge of the foot, which is the reflex area to the spine. As you move upward, press downward with your fingers so that the foot twists and the webbing of the working hand presses on the inner edge of the foot. Move both hands

up toward the toes slightly, and repeat this twisting action.

When you reach the top of the foot, continue the same movement while moving down toward the heel. Stimulating the full length of the inner edge of the foot can relax the entire spine.

Kneading

This easy relaxation technique is great for improving circulation. Kneading is one technique that requires the use of both hands. Place both hands on either side of the foot, with the thumbs on top and the fingers underneath. Work your

fingers into the fleshy part of the sole, as if you are kneading bread. Move your hands up and down the foot. Then you can reverse your hand so that the thumbs are on the bottom. Work your thumbs in a kneading motion up and down the sole.

Thumb-Crossing

This technique stimulates the bottoms of the feet, and requires both hands. Place the hands on either side of the foot, with the thumbs on the soles and the fingers on the top. Criss—cross your thumbs horizontally across the foot, beginning at the

heel and moving up toward the toes and then back down. As your thumbs slide from side to side, apply steady pressure and try to touch the foot from edge to edge.

"V" Thumb Slide

Similar to "thumb–crossing," this technique stimulates the sole of the foot with both hands. Place the hands on either side of the foot, with the thumbs on the soles and the fingers on top. Beginning at the heel, alternate your thumbs as they move outward and upward, from the middle of the foot, at about a 45–degree angle. When you reach the toes,

continue this movement back down
to the heel.

Solar Plexus Relaxer

The solar plexus is the "nerve
switchboard" of the body, and by
relaxing its reflex area you can relax
the entire body. To locate the solar
plexus reflex, hold the top of the foot
with the fingers of one hand, and
gently squeeze the sides of the foot
together so the surface of the sole
wrinkles. You'll notice a vertical
wrinkle in the center of the foot. At
the base of this wrinkle, which is
normally at the base of the ball of
the foot, lies the solar plexus reflex.

Hold the heel with your supporting hand, and press the thumb of your working hand into this area and hold. As your partner inhales, press into the foot, and on the exhalation, release the pressure. Repeat this a couple of times.

To stimulate the solar plexus even deeper, place both thumbs on the solar plexus reflex and gently bend the toes toward you by pressing your fingers downward on the top of the foot. As the foot bends, your thumbs will sink deep into the solar plexus. Release pressure on the exhalation, and apply pressure on the inhalation.

Finger Pressure

Stimulate specific reflex areas on the foot by holding the heel of the foot with one hand and using your thumb to apply steady, static pressure to different points. Hold each reflex area for five seconds and release. Ask your partner to inhale and apply pressure on the inhalation. On the exhalation, release the pressure. You can also make small

circles with your thumb on each reflex area. To do this, apply pressure with your thumb, and then keep it in the same spot while moving your hand in a circular motion. Rather than moving the thumb around to "rub" the foot, you're focusing your energy and pressure on one reflex point and almost vibrating or pulsating the point of pressure.

Thumb-Walking

This technique allows you to stimulate larger areas on the foot and affect whole body systems, rather than just specific reflex points. Hold

the heel with your supporting hand and place your thumb on the reflex area you'd like to affect. Using an "inchworm" movement, bend the thumb at the first joint and inch your thumb up the foot slowly. The walking movement is always forward, never backward. To thumb-walk the entire foot, I recommend dividing the foot into five sections by the horizontal lines (pelvic, waist, diaphragm, and neck/shoulder lines). When you reach the top of a section, bring your thumb back to the line where you started, move the thumb over to the next zone and inch upward. You can cover the

entire foot with this technique.

The Ending

After you complete a foot treatment, use both hands to "brush" the negative energy out of the foot. Alternating hands, brush your fingertips on the bottom of the foot, from the heel to the toes, and on the top of the foot, from the ankle to the toes. Do this several times on each side of the foot. To end a treatment, place both hands on the foot or feet, and hold them here for a few seconds. This is very relaxing and can enhance the reflexology experience. After you do this, you may want to

shake your hands and then wash
them with soap and water to get rid
of any leftover negative energy. If
you're wearing shoes or socks, you
may also want to touch the floor
with your hands to ground yourself.
If you're barefoot, the soles of your
feet will "ground" excess energy.

Part IV

Reflexology
for the
Body Systems

Another approach for a reflexology treatment is to focus on one particular body system that may be out of balance and in need of attention. Stimulating all of the body's ten systems can strengthen and balance the system so that it functions as effectively as possible.

1. Circulatory System

The circulatory system consists of the heart, blood vessels, and blood. More than 1,000 times a day, blood

circulates in one direction through the body's 60,000-mile network of veins and arteries. The heart is responsible for pumping oxygen into the blood and collecting carbon dioxide that is expelled through the lungs.

Approximately 24,000 gallons of blood pass through the heart daily. Red blood cells carry oxygen, minerals, nutrients, hormones, and antibodies to every cell through their 120-day life span, and, along with white blood cells, fight disease. When stress and tension build up in the body, circulation becomes sluggish, the cardiovascular system tightens up, and blood flow is

restricted. It's extremely important to manage your stress levels so that the cardiovascular system can conduct a smooth flow of blood throughout the body.

Reflex areas to stimulate:

👉 **Heart:** Use finger pressure on the heart reflex, located on the left foot.

👉 **Blood vessels and blood:** Knead, thumb-cross, and "V" slide over the soles of both feet.

2. Digestive System

The digestive system consists of a

group of organs that break food down into tiny nutrients so they can be absorbed and converted into energy for the body. This system also builds and replaces cells and tissue. The digestive system begins in the mouth, continues in the pharynx (throat) and esophagus, and extends into the "gut" region, which includes the stomach, the small and large intestines, the rectum, and the anus. As food passes through the body, it is mixed with numerous digestive juices, which break it down into smaller units that can be absorbed into the blood and lymphatic systems. Some are used for

energy, some as building blocks for tissues and cells, and some are stored for future or emergency use. The liver and the pancreas also secrete digestive juices that break down food as it passes through the digestive ducts. Since not everything that we eat can be digested, waste is then sent through the colon and out of the body. The digestive system is comprised of the mouth, teeth, tongue, throat, esophagus, stomach, pancreas, duodenum, liver, gall bladder, small intestine, colon, and ileocecal valve.

Reflex areas to stimulate:

☞ **Mouth, teeth, tongue, throat, and esophagus:** Finger–walk up the entire section between the neck/shoulder line and the tops of the feet. Use finger pressure on the big toe, the reflex to the neck/throat.

☞ **Stomach, pancreas, duodenum, liver, gall bladder, small intestine, colon, and ileocecal valve:** Thumb-cross and finger-walk up the sections between the pelvic line and the diaphragm line.

3. Endocrine System

The endocrine system is a collection of glands that produce the hormones necessary for normal bodily functions. These hormones are responsible for a wide variety of physiological processes, including regulating metabolism, growth, sexual development, emotions, and energy levels. They help the body maintain homeostasis, a state of chemical and emotional balance. The endocrine glands release hormones directly into the bloodstream, where they are transported to organs and tissues throughout the entire body. The endocrine glands regulate the

functioning of all the body's systems. The endocrine system is comprised of the hypothalamus, pineal, pituitary, thyroid, parathyroid, thymus, adrenals, pancreas, ovaries in women, and testes in men.

Reflex areas to stimulate:

Hypothalamus, pineal, pituitary, thyroid, and parathyroid: Thumb–walk and use finger pressure on the big toe. Work the entire toe, from the base to the top and on both sides.

Thymus, adrenals, and pancreas: Finger–walk the

area between the waist line
and the diaphragm line.

☞ **Ovaries in women and
testes in men:** Use finger
pressure on the area just
below the anklebone, on the
outside of both feet. Add
some gentle, circular motion
to the finger pressure.

4. Lymphatic System

The lymphatic system, which is
essential to the body's defense
mechanisms, filters out organisms
that cause disease, produces certain
white blood cells, and generates
antibodies. It's also important for the

distribution of fluids and nutrients in the body, because it drains excess fluids and protein so that tissues do not swell up. The lymphatic vessels are present wherever there are blood vessels, and they transport excess fluid to the end vessels without the assistance of any "pumping" action. The lymphatic system and the cardiovascular system are closely related structures that are joined by a capillary system. The body is able to eliminate the products of cellular breakdown and bacterial invasion through blood flow, the lymph nodes, and into the lymph.

There are more than one hundred

lymph nodes, located mainly in the neck, groin, armpits, and scattered all along the lymph vessels. These act as barriers to infection by filtering out and destroying toxins and germs. The largest body of lymphoid tissue is the spleen. Two significant parts of the lymphatic system are the right lymphatic duct, which drains lymph fluid from the upper right quarter of the body above the diaphragm and down the midline, and the thoracic duct, which drains the rest of the body. It is through the actions of this system that our body is able to fight infection and to ward off foreign invaders. The lymphatic

system is comprised of the lymph vessels and ducts, lymph nodes and fluid, spleen, tonsils, thymus, and appendix.

Reflex areas to stimulate:
Lymph vessels and ducts, lymph nodes and fluid: Knead and thumb–cross both feet.

Spleen, tonsils, thymus, and appendix: Use finger pressure on each of these reflex areas.

5. Muscular System

The muscular system includes over six hundred muscles of the

body. Muscles, which are attached to bones by tendons and other tissues, exert force by converting chemical energy into tension and contraction. They are made up of millions of tiny protein filaments that work together, contracting and releasing, to produce motion in the body. Every single muscle in the body is connected to the brain and spinal cord by nerves. Muscles have many functions, and so we are equipped with three types of muscle: cardiac muscles, found only in the heart, which power the pumping action; smooth muscles, which surround or are part of the internal

organs; and skeletal muscles, which are the muscles we use to move our bodies. Cardiac and smooth muscles are involuntary and are not under any conscious control. The skeletal muscles, on the other hand, carry out voluntary move-ments. They are the body's most abundant tissue, as they comprise about twenty–three percent of a woman's body weight and about forty percent of a man's body weight. The muscular system includes the heart, diaphragm, and intestinal walls.

Reflex areas to stimulate:
👉 **600 muscles:** Knead and finger–walk the entire foot.

👉 **Heart, diaphragm:** Use finger pressure on these reflex areas.

👉 **Intestinal walls:** Finger-walk the area between the pelvic line and the waist line.

6. Nervous System

The central nervous system is the body's information gatherer, storage center, and control system. Its overall function is to collect information about the body's external state, to analyze this information, and to respond appropriately to satisfy certain needs, the most powerful of which is survival. The nerves do not

form one single system, but several interrelated systems. The brain and spinal cord make up the central nervous system. The peripheral nervous system is responsible for the body functions that are not under conscious control, such as your heartbeat or digestive system.

The nervous system uses electrical impulses, which travel along the length of the cells. Each cell processes information from the sensory nerves and initiates an action within milliseconds. These impulses travel at speeds up to 250 miles per hour, while other systems, such as the endocrine, may take many hours

to respond with hormones. The nervous system is comprised of the brain (including the hypothalamus, pituitary, and pineal glands), spinal cord, and solar plexus.

Reflex areas to stimulate:

☞ **Brain (including the hypothalamus, pituitary, and pineal glands):** Finger–walk the entire big toe, from the base of the toe to the top, and on both sides.

☞ **Spinal cord:** Finger–walk along the inside edge of the foot, from the heel to the base of the big toe.

👉 **Solar plexus:** Use the Solar Plexus Relaxer technique.

7. Reproductive System

The male reproductive system consists of the penis, seminal vesicles, vas deferens, prostate, and testes. This system enables a man to fertilize a woman's eggs with sperm. Sperm, along with male sex hormones, is produced in the testes, a pair of oval–shaped glands that are suspended in a pouch called the scrotum. The male sexual organs are partly visible and partly hidden within the body. The visible parts are the penis and the scrotum. Inside the

body are the prostate gland and tubes, which link the system together. The male organs produce and transfer sperm to the female for fertilization.

The female reproductive system consists of the vagina, uterus, fallopian tubes, ovaries, and mammary glands. These organs enable a woman to produce eggs, to nourish and house a fertilized egg until it is fully developed, and to give birth. Unlike the male, the female sexual organs are almost entirely hidden.

Reflex areas to stimulate:
Men: Penis, seminal vesi-

cles, vas deferens, prostate, and testes.

Women: Vagina, uterus, fallopian tubes, ovaries, and mammary glands.

☞ For both men and women: Use finger pressure on the inside and outside of each foot, just under the anklebone. On each foot, finger–walk along the pathway over the top of the foot that connects the anklebones.

8. Respiratory System

Healthy functioning of the respiratory system is necessary for survival.

The respiratory system contains those organs that are responsible for carrying oxygen from the air to the bloodstream and expelling the waste product—carbon dioxide. Breathing, like the beat of one's heart, is an automatic function that is controlled by the brain. Respir-ation is the act of burning energy from oxygen. Breathing is an obvious part of the respiratory flow, but the flow of energy and air is also involved in yawning, sneezing, coughing, hic-cuping, speaking, and sensing smell. The respiratory flow is also chan-neled to the larynx, or voice box, which uses it to create a range of

sounds so that humans can communicate vocally. The respiratory system is comprised of the nose, sinuses, lungs, and diaphragm.

Reflex areas to stimulate:
Nose and sinuses:
Finger–walk all of the toes. Use finger pressure on the tops of each toe.

Lungs and diaphragm:
Finger-walk the area between the diaphragm line and neck/shoulder line.

9. Skeletal System
The average adult human skeleton

has 206 bones that store minerals such as calcium, which can be supplied to other parts of the body. The bones are joined to ligaments and tendons to form a protective, supportive framework for the attached muscles and the soft tissues that underlie it. The skeleton plays an important part in movement by providing a series of independently movable levers, which the muscles can pull to move different parts of the body. The skeleton also produces red blood cells from the bone marrow of certain bones, and produces white blood cells from the marrow of other bones to destroy harmful bacteria.

The skeleton consists of the skull, the spine, the ribs, the sternum (breastbone), the shoulders, the pelvis, and their attached limb bones. Babies are born with 270 soft bones—about sixty-four more than adults; many of these fuse together by around the age of twenty into the 206 hard, permanent bones.

Reflex areas to stimulate:
All the bones of the body: Knead and finger-walk the entire foot.

10. Urinary System

The urinary system is a little like a plumbing system, with special pipes that allow water and salts to flow through them. The structure of the urinary tract includes the kidneys, two ureters (tubes leading from the kidneys to the bladder), and the urethra, a tube leading from the bladder to the exterior of the body. The kidneys make up a filter system for the blood, reabsorbing almost ninety-nine percent of the fluid into it, and sending only two to four pints of waste, or urine, into the bladder for storage until it

can be disposed of. The kidneys allow the blood to maintain glucose, salts, and minerals after cleansing it of toxins that will be passed out through the urinary tract.

Reflex areas to stimulate: Kidneys, bladder, ureter tubes, and urethra: Finger–walk the area between the pelvic line and the waist line. Use finger pressure on the reflex area to the kidneys and bladder.

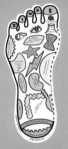

Sole-utions

One of the best things about reflexology is how easily you can incorporate it into your daily life.

Reflexology offers an easy and quick way to get the benefits of a full body massage—and you don't even have to take off your clothes! You can do reflexology almost anywhere, anytime, and you don't need anyone to help you. Use it when you are traveling or in need of quick relief at work. Use it to heal yourself, your family, a friend, a child—even a pet. Here is a

list of common problems and the reflex areas to stimulate to provide relief.

Acne
Reflex areas: Liver, kidneys, bladder, small intestine

Alcoholism/ Chemical Dependency
Reflex areas: Brain, liver, kidney, solar plexus

Allergies
Reflex areas: Lungs, sinuses, eyes, thymus

Anemia
Reflex areas: Spleen, liver, heart, lungs

Anxiety
Reflex areas: Solar plexus, stomach, brain

Arthritis
Reflex areas: Kidneys, liver, adrenal glands

Asthma
Reflex areas: Lungs, solar plexus, thymus, adrenals

Autoimmunity Disorders
(See also multiple sclerosis)
Reflex areas: Thymus, adrenals, solar plexus

Back Pain
Reflex areas: Spine, neck, shoulders, brain

Bladder Infections
(See also urinary tract infections)
Reflex areas: Bladder, kidneys, ureters

Carpal Tunnel Syndrome (CTS)
Reflex areas: Brain, lungs, solar plexus

Chronic Fatigue Syndrome (CFS)
Reflex areas: Adrenals, brain, pituitary, solar plexus

Colds and Flu
Reflex areas: Thyroid, thymus, lungs, sinuses, eyes

Colic
Reflex areas: Stomach, colon, small intestine

Colon Problems
Reflex areas: Colon, small intestine, stomach, solar plexus

Dandruff
Reflex areas: Kidneys, thyroid, adrenals, solar plexus

Depression
Reflex areas: Adrenals, brain, pituitary, pineal, heart, thyroid

Digestion Problems
Reflex areas: Stomach, neck, solar plexus

Ear Problems
Reflex areas: Ears, neck, thymus, solar plexus

Emphysema
Reflex areas: Lungs, neck, solar plexus

Eye Problems
Reflex areas: Eyes, brain, kidneys, thymus

Gastrointestinal Problems:
Constipation
Reflex areas: Colon, small intestine, stomach, brain

Diarrhea
Reflex areas: Stomach, small intestine, colon, kidneys

Foot Pain:

A relaxing foot rub can help minimize agony due to foot pain. To relieve any of the following problems, stimulate the entire foot, and then follow the suggestions for other soothing sole-utions:

Problem	Symptom	Other Soothing Sole-utions
Bunions	A bony bump at the base of the big toe	Apply ice. Avoid high heels.
Calluses	Patches of hardened or thickened skin	Soak feet in warm water to soften skin, then use pumice stone
Corns	Red, thick areas of skin on tops or between toes	Follow sole-ution for calluses. Try over-the-counter corn pads.

Hammertoes	Painful, curled, claw-like toes	Wear wide, comfortable shoes. Use over-the-counter pads.
Plantar Fasciitis	Arch and/or heel pain that feels like a bruise.	This is an inflammation of the ligament of the sole. Apply ice; wear well-cushioned shoes.
Ingrown toenail	Pain and swelling near edge of toenail.	Soak feet in warm water. Avoid over-trimming corners, which can cause nails to grow into the skin.
Neuroma	Pain and numbness on the ball of the foot, into the toes	Place a pad in shoes under the ball between the third and fourth toes. Wear wide, soft shoes.

Hair (thinning or baldness)
Reflex areas: Thyroid, pituitary, lungs

Hangovers
Reflex areas: Liver, kidneys, stomach, solar plexus

Headaches
(See also migraines)
Reflex areas: Brain, eyes, neck, shoulders, back, solar plexus

Hemorrhoids
Reflex areas: Hemorrhoids, colon, adrenals

Hernia
Reflex areas: Stomach, lungs, neck

High Blood Pressure
Reflex areas: Adrenals, brain, solar plexus

High Cholesterol
Reflex areas: Heart, liver, solar plexus, thyroid

High Energy
Reflex areas: Solar plexus, stomach, brain

Hypoglycemia

Reflex areas: Pituitary, adrenals, thyroid, liver

Immunity Problems

Reflex areas: Thymus, spleen, pituitary, brain

Infertility

Reflex areas: Hypothalamus, reproductive organs, solar plexus, spine

Inflammation

Reflex areas: Adrenals, thymus, spleen

Insomnia

Reflex areas: Brain, thyroid, pineal, pituitary, solar plexus

Jet Lag

Reflex areas: Brain, pineal, pituitary, spine

Kidney Problems

Reflex areas: Kidneys, bladder, ureters, spine (lower back), thymus

Knee Problems

Reflex areas: Knee, spine, adrenals

Liver Problems
Reflex areas: Liver, lungs, small intestine

Low Energy
Reflex areas: Brain, thymus, pituitary, thyroid

Menopause
Reflex areas: Sex organs (ovaries, uterus, fallopian tubes), solar plexus, thyroid, brain

Migraines
(See also headaches)
Reflex areas: Brain, pituitary, eyes, stomach, solar plexus

Motion Sickness
Reflex areas: Stomach, ears, eyes

Multiple Sclerosis
(See also autoimmune disorders)
Reflex areas: Adrenals, thymus, thyroid, brain, spine

Nausea
Reflex areas: Stomach, small intestine, inner ear, brain

Neck Pain
Reflex areas: Neck, spine, adrenals, solar plexus

Osteoporosis

Reflex areas: Adrenals, heart, pituitary, small intestine

Premenstrual Syndrome

Reflex areas: Sex organs (uterus, ovaries, fallopian tubes), brain, thyroid, stomach, solar plexus

Psoriasis

Reflex areas: Small intestine, kidneys, liver, thyroid

Sexual Problems

Sex is everywhere—in advertisements for cigarettes, automobiles, and fast-food restaurants. In short, sex sells. Within everyone there exists a dynamic drive for reproducing the human species that motivates much of our everyday behavior. For some people, the sex drive is so intense that it rates second only to oxygen for survival requirements! It is one of the strongest animal drives, and it cannot be ignored.

For those experiencing problems in the sexual arena, help is here! Reflexology offers drug-free relief

for sluggish or diminishing sex drives by stimulating the reflex areas that are directly responsible for the overall health and well–being of the body, increasing your sex drive and hormone production and slowing the aging process.

Reflexology can also bring enhanced "touch" into a relation-ship, which is important to intimacy and the development of a deep emo-tional connection. All couples must learn to communicate their desires and feelings to each other in every aspect of their lives. In the sexual arena, communication is the key to happiness. Reflexology can help

couples learn to communicate honestly with each other and be sensitive to a partner's feelings. Reflexology is also a great way to spice up your sex life by learning how to tune into each other's body and provide intimate physical pleasure.

The reflexology points for sexual problems vary by problem. Those experiencing a low sex drive will want to focus on endocrine glands (including the thyroid, pituitary, pineal, thymus, adrenals, ovaries, and testes) which are responsible for secreting hormones and releasing them into the body. Of these, the thyroid and adrenals are the most

important to boost your sex drive and improve sexual functioning for both men and women. Additionally, stimulating the reflex areas for sexual organs strengthens both the organ itself as well as your sex drive.

Those struggling with the problem of impotency can use reflexology to help restore these important abilities and improve the levels of testosterone in the body. In this case, working the adrenal glands, pituitary, thyroid, and sex organs is recommended as well as the prostate, testes, and vas deferens.

For prostate problems, stimulate adrenal glands to produce an ade-

quate amount of hormones, the sex organs, the bladder (to eliminate toxins), and the ureters to prevent infections. On the other hand, if you find your sex life is affected by stress, then you'll want to work the solar plexus and brain—not just for yourself but for your partner! Stimulating the solar plexus area is a great way to calm down, and working the brain center restores mental and physical harmony for all parties.

Sinus Problems

Reflex areas: Sinuses, lungs, pituitary

Smoking

Reflex areas: Brain, lungs, solar plexus

Snoring (sleep apnea)

Reflex areas: Adrenals, lungs, spleen

Swollen Ankles and Feet

Reflex areas: Adrenals, bladder, kidneys, ureters

Tendonitis

Reflex areas: Adrenals, Achilles tendon

Thyroid Problems

Reflex areas: Thyroid, neck, solar plexus

Toothache

Reflex areas: Sinuses, neck, brain, adrenals

Ulcers

Reflex areas: Stomach, thymus, thyroid

Urinary Tract Infections
(See also bladder infections)
Reflex areas: Bladder, kidneys, ureters

Warts and Corns
Reflex areas: Thymus, pituitary, spleen

Weight Problems
Reflex areas:
To lose weight: Thyroid, pineal, pituitary, liver, colon, kidneys
To gain weight: Thyroid, solar plexus, stomach, brain

This book has been bound
using handcraft methods and
Smyth-sewn to ensure durability.

The dust jacket and interior were
illustrated by Sheila Smallwood
and Carolyn Reyes

The dust jacket was designed
by Mary Ann Liquori

The interior was designed
by Serrin Bodmer.

The text was edited
by Nancy Armstrong

The text was set
in Estro and Trebuchet MS.

CW00400143